Safety & Security for Travellers

A pocket book & field guide
for people on the move

Martin Akhurst

First Edition 2015

Published by:
Fieldcraft Solutions, Barnoldswick, United Kingdom
books@fieldcraft.co.uk
www.fieldcraft.co.uk

ISBN 978-0-9934082-0-5

CONTENTS

Preface   1

Travel Safety   3

Other People   11

On the Move   17

Crime   29

Hostile Environments & Weapons of War   49

Field First Aid   63

Surviving Natural Disasters   77

Communications   85

Appendix   93

Notes   111

Emergency Contacts   117

PREFACE

This pocket book provides useful tips and advice for people on the move for work, study or leisure.

Travel can be demanding and stressful but a few simple precautions can make for a better experience. A positive attitude to safety can also help the traveller to achieve their goals and avoid unnecessary difficulties.

A challenge for any book on safety & security is to maintain a balanced perspective, highlighting problems without deterring the would be traveller from their objectives. Incidents of violence and hostility are still relatively rare and extreme threats are largely limited to a few hotspots around the world.

Nevertheless, incidents can be traumatic, may affect many people besides the immediate victim, delay projects, ruin holidays and destroy lives.

No guide can anticipate all situations, but by following a few simple procedures and adapting them to your own situation, you should be able to travel safely and enjoy your time away.

Disclaimer

While every effort is made to ensure that the information contained in this publication is accurate, the author and publisher can accept no liability for any inaccuracies that may occur or the consequences arising from them.

TRAVEL SAFETY

Preparing to go

A point of contact

Packing for your trip

Clothing

Air travel

Hotel & hostel safety

Urban safety

PREPARING TO GO

Time spent preparing for a trip can avoid a lot of problems later on. It is useful to have a checklist to ensure that nothing is overlooked.

Example - Pre-trip Checklist

- Passport is valid and up to date
- Visa correct for the destination
- Tickets for travel
- Medical - e.g.:
  - Fit to travel
  - Personal prescription medications
  - Yellow fever and/or other required certificates
  - Malaria Prophylaxis
  - Insect repellent/mosquito net
- Foreign currency and travel insurance
- Addresses for key destinations
  - E.g. hotels, local contacts, embassy, etc.
- Back up copies of important documents
  - Photocopies
  - Encrypted and emailed to a secure address
- Security clearance
- Home contact advised of travel plans
- Clothing suitable for the climate
- Personal first aid kit
- Suitable luggage (suitcases, rucksacks, etc.)
- Mobile/cell phone with roaming SIM card

A POINT OF CONTACT

It is important that someone at home or work knows that you are travelling, acts as a point of contact and is able to help if there is an emergency.

Does your home/work contact know..?

- That you are going
- Where you are going
- How you will contact them
- How they can contact you
- That you have arrived at your destination
- Who you are planning to stay with
- How often you will check in
- What to do if you do not check in or go missing

It is important to choose the right person to act as your point of contact. They must be reliable, understand what to do in an emergency and be available for the duration of your trip. It is best to meet with your contact before travelling and discuss their responsibilities.

Ensure that the contact has all your relevant details, e.g.

- Personal details and next of kin
- Contacts at your destination
- Copies of insurance documents
- Travel Itinerary...

...and make sure that you know how to contact them at any time of day.

PACKING FOR YOUR TRIP

When boarding an aircraft, put essential items in your cabin/carry-on bag. This will include things that allow you to survive if your other luggage goes missing or is delayed.

Cabin luggage

Carry essential items and valuables with you at all times. A small, tough rucksack is ideal:

- Small wash kit
- Personal medicines
- Passport/ID cards
- Emergency contact list
- Phone and charger
- Local currency
- Change of clothes
- Waterproof, lightweight jacket
- Small torch

Hold-luggage

When choosing hold-luggage, consider where you will need to carry it and take the smallest bag you can manage. Look for something strong and secure.

Money Belts

These are good for protecting larger sums of money but it is important to keep smaller amounts of cash to hand so you do not have to open the money belt in public.

CLOTHING

What to wear?

Clothes and footwear must be right for the climate and the culture that you are visiting. Clothes that can be easily washed and dried may also be useful.

Choose clothes that are comfortable - being too hot, too cold or having sore feet will spoil your trip and may also distract you from other possible hazards.

Wear clothes that will not offend local customs but do not try to look like a local unless you really can. Consider cultural sensitivities and take at least some clothes that will allow you to cover your arms and legs. In some countries, women may need to wear a head scarf.

Consider what your clothing says about you: Respectful visitor? Wealthy traveller? Naïve fool? Avoid clothes of a military design or colour that may bring you unwanted attention.

If you are working, find out what clothes are respected in the local business or civil culture. If you are in any doubt, it is generally better to be a little more formal rather than too casual, particularly if you want people to take you seriously. First impressions can make all the difference.

Pockets that can be fastened securely, and inside pockets on jackets, provide more protection from thieves. Some clothing designed for travellers will have concealed pockets for valuable items such as passports and credit cards.

AIR TRAVEL

Thinking ahead can prevent many of the common but avoidable problems faced by travellers at this initial stage of their journey.

Before you depart

- Who will meet you at the airport and where?
- How will they identify themselves?
- What will they do if your flight is delayed...
    - Wait at the airport?
    - Go home until you call?
- What if your flight is delayed and they they cannot meet you when you arrive?
- What is their contact number?
- Who at home knows your flight details?
- Is there a better time of day/night to arrive?
- Are there any security issues at the airport?

Arriving at an airport

- Know where you are going (e.g. which hotel)
- If meeting someone for the first time, confirm that they are who they say they are

Airport taxis

- Use only official taxis
- What currency do they accept for payment?
- What is the normal fare to your hotel?
- What is the normal journey time

HOTEL & HOSTEL SAFETY

Accommodation is where many people feel most vulnerable while travelling. Researching the best places, looking after possessions and being aware of the environment can help maintain safety & security.

- Choose a hotel in a safe area of town
- Ask for a room that is 1 or 2 levels above the street
- Check the route to the fire exit and put a label on the back of your door to show the direction of escape
- Carry a door wedge to put under the door while you are sleeping or washing
- Meet visitors in reception rather than in your room
- If an unexpected caller knocks on your door, ask them to meet you in reception
- If using hotel Wi-Fi connections, make sure you log on to the correct access point – check the name
- Do not leave keys lying around to prevent other people seeing your room number
- Assume that your room is not secure and leave valuables elsewhere, e.g. in the hotel safe. Carry a small padlock in case there are lockers available
- Be aware of the area around the hotel. Is it safe? Are there street lights? Etc.

A good hotel or hostel will take an interest in your well-being but if you are unsure do not hesitate to find somewhere else. You will not rest and relax if your are anxious.

URBAN SAFETY

Urban areas can be complex, busy environments. A wise traveller will be alert to the situation around them and sensitive to who is nearby. Try to avoid going out alone but if you are in a group, make sure that everybody knows where to meet if you are separated.

- Plan the route you will take before you depart
- If you are lost, step into a safe place rather than standing on the pavement to look at your map
- Carry possessions in a plain bag with a strap that you can put over your shoulder and across your body
- If you are concerned about being followed out of a café or at an ATM, etc. walk a few metres in one direction before turning around to go another way, you may notice if anyone is following you as they will also have to change direction
- Walk confidently – muggers and other criminals are looking for 'vulnerable' people
- Carry important contact details including the address of your hotel, embassy, etc.
- If you are taking photographs, be careful not to infringe any laws or customs. In some countries it is illegal to photograph government and military buildings
- If you are sightseeing, get into the habit of briefly looking around you to see what is happening before you stop to enjoy the views

OTHER PEOPLE

Cultural differences
Building relationships
Managing your team
Diffusing anger

CULTURAL DIFFERENCES

Meeting people from another culture is one of the great pleasures of travel. However, it is important to avoid assumptions and to adapt to new ways of doing things. It is better to begin by being too polite then relaxing as you learn what is acceptable, this way you will not offend anyone before you understand social norms and customs

Across cultures

- Listen and observe, avoid assumptions
- Do not be afraid to ask what is acceptable
- Remember that whether you are on holiday or on business, you are in another person's home country
- Spend some time learning about the culture before your visit

Language barriers

- Use plain language
- Avoid jargon
- Speak a little more slowly than normal
- Do not speak to someone like a child just because they do not speak your language fluently
- Learn at least a few words of the local language
- Confirm that you have understood each other by repeating what you think has been agreed and/or asking the other person to do the same
- Write down a few useful phrases in the local language

BUILDING RELATIONSHIPS

When staying in the same area for any length of time, think about introducing yourself to people who might be helpful in an emergency. Build a network of contacts that you can rely upon.

- Register with your embassy or consulate - they may advise or assist you in the event of an emergency
- Consider introducing yourself to the local authorities, e.g. "I am here teaching English for 6 months and just came to say hello"
- Letters of introduction from senior figures and requests to allow you safe passage can be useful in areas with travel restrictions
- Hotel staff can be a good source of local information about places to see, places to avoid, reliable taxi companies, how to deal with the police, etc.
- If you have a driver or other local person in your group, use their knowledge to help you understand the area; where to go and where to avoid, local customs, useful contacts, etc.
- If your visit involves helping local people, explaining this to appropriate individuals and agencies will help you to be accepted and can bring many benefits

There may be times when you come in to contact with individuals who are hostile to your presence, even here, attempting to build a better relationship can make your life easier.

MANAGING YOUR TEAM

If you are travelling within a group or leading a team of people then safety & security means ensuring that everyone understands what is acceptable and safe behaviour. This can be achieved by involving other people in agreeing what is acceptable and unacceptable behaviour and briefing everyone on any risks

- Explain clearly what is expected from individuals
- Ask questions to confirm understanding
- Explain why any specific security procedures are needed and how they will help
- Meet together to discuss any issues...
- ...and also try and talk to individuals about any particular concerns that they may have
- Develop an appropriate movement monitoring plan so that other members of the group can be easily contacted and traced
- Discuss what will happen if there is an incident
- Encourage people to look out for each other
- Update the group regularly and check that everybody is still following the agreed procedures

Encourage people to think not just about their own well-being but about the wider implications of a safety or security incident such as the impact on colleagues and relatives or on the project that they are involved in. Some people will take more risks than others and it is important to agree what is tolerable for the group as a whole.

DIFFUSING ANGER

Anger is usually the result of fear or frustration - it does not always mean a person will become aggressive. An angry person may not be able to think clearly, so avoid asking them complex questions. Diffusing the anger may have to occur before the underlying problem can be dealt with.

Dealing with anger

- Calm yourself – try to take some deep breathes
- Be careful of your own body language
- Do not point and avoid crossing your arms
- Allow more personal space than usual
- Show concern and a willingness to help
- Ask the person to describe *what* has upset them?
- If the person is being very loud or talking quickly, talk a little less loudly and quickly and then gradually reduce the volume/speed of your own voice – they may do the same
- Show respect – even if you do not feel it
- Try to suggest a way forward
- Avoid trying to prove that the other person is wrong

Some signs of aggression

- High levels of agitation
- Clenching of fists, head down
- Gritting teeth
- Staring as if selecting targets

ON THE MOVE

Death & injury on the road

Inspecting a vehicle

Vehicle equipment

Driver skills check-list

Taxis

Buses & coaches

Checkpoints

Driving in convoy

Armoured vehicles

DEATH & INJURY ON THE ROAD

Travel by car can be one of the most hazardous things that we do. Figures from the World Health Organisation show that there are on average 9.3 deaths for every 100,000 vehicles on the road. However, when looked at on a country level, it is clear that this is a much bigger problem in some countries than others

Deaths per 100,000 vehicles

Global Mean	**9.3**
Ethiopia	11,666
DRC	6440
Afghanistan	1447
U.S.A.	15
France	12
United Kingdom	7
Germany	4.2

Principal causes of death

- Driving too fast
- Not wearing a seatbelt
- Driving inappropriately for the road conditions

In addition to accidents, security incidents are also more likely to occur while travelling. It is good practice to plan your itinerary so as to reduce the number of journeys you make to a minimum.

INSPECTING A VEHICLE

A few simple checks each time you use a vehicle should be part of your safety routine

F.L.O.W.E.R.

F   Fuel

- Do you have enough for a **return** journey?

L   Lights

- Are they working? Are any broken?

O   Oil

- Is there any sign of a leak?
- look for patches of oil under the engine

W   Water

- Is the radiator leaking?
- Is there water for the windscreen washers?

E   Electrics

- Do the locks and windows work?
- Does the battery warning light go out when the engine is running? If not, the battery will discharge while you drive

R   Rubber (tires)

- Are they all equally inflated?
- Can you see any cuts, abrasions or bulges in the side wall? Is the tread depth adequate?

VEHICLE EQUIPMENT

It is impossible to provide a definitive list of what to take on a journey but the following items may be needed.

For the vehicle

- Spare tyres x 2
- Tools
- Spare fuel
- Jack and wheel spanner
- Tow rope
- Light bulbs and fuses
- Engine oil and water
- Fire extinguisher
- Warning triangle...

For the passengers

- Paperwork/travel documents
- Radio
- Torch and batteries
- First aid kit
- Water
- Blankets
- Food
- Map and compass...

Ensure that all items are securely stowed so that they do not become a danger in the event of an accident or crash

DRIVER SKILLS CHECK-LIST

Skill	Required	✓
- General Training		
- Specialist Training		
- General Mechanics		
- Knowledge of Area		
- Navigation		
- Car-jack response		
- Ambush/crossfire response		
- Checkpoint training		
- Armoured vehicle driving		
- Convoy driving		
- Radio communication		
- Security record check		
- Language skills		

Caring for your driver

If you have a driver, it is important to consider their welfare and ensure that they have adequate breaks. In conflict areas, make sure you do not ask them to visit somewhere that would put them at risk, such as a region that is in conflict with their own people.

TAXIS

Using a taxi puts your safety in the hands of a stranger. Choose carefully and if in doubt don't get into the vehicle.

- Use a reputable company (ask at the hotel)
- Tell someone where you are going
- If you do not want people to know where you live, meet the taxi at a nearby location
- Always wear a seatbelt
- Sit in the back of the taxi and remain alert
- Don't show all your cash when paying the fare
- Carry small notes and coins to avoid the inevitable problem of, "*Sorry, I don't have any change*"
- Ask the driver to stop if you do not feel safe

If the driver goes too fast

- Ask them to slow down
- If possible, tell them you will have to report them
- Ask the taxi driver to stop, pay the fare and leave
- If they ignore your request, try telling them that the speed/fear will make you vomit in the vehicle!

If you fear that you are being abducted

You could try to use your phone (or pretend) and say:

- "*Hi. I'm on my way, we are just passing through* [describe where you are]. *Look out for my taxi; it's a* [colour and make]. *You will recognize the driver, they are* [sex, age, distinguishing features]*"

BUSES & COACHES

Public transport and private coaches can be a great way to travel, it is often the cheapest option, however they are also environments where petty crime is common.

At the terminal

The areas around bus and coach stations are notorious places for pick-pockets and bag thieves.

- Keep a close check on your possessions and remain alert to who is around you
- If possible, wait in a less busy, but safe area

On the bus/coach

- Have small change to pay the fare
- Before you board the vehicle, ask yourself if it, and the driver, are in good condition?
- Keep bags close to you, away from the aisle
- Keep your passport/visa, etc. on your person
- Watch out for pick-pockets
- If your bag is in a luggage compartment, be alert at stops in case someone takes it off the coach
- Wear a seatbelt if it is provided
- Keep valuables in an inside pocket of the clothes that you are wearing
- If you want to sleep, lie against your bag/possessions to prevent tampering
- Try to avoid having to sit at the front of the vehicle as this will often be the worst affected area in a crash

CHECKPOINTS

Awareness & preparation

- Who operates the checkpoints?
- Where are the checkpoints?
- What are the normal procedures?
  - E.g. documents required, fees, etc.
- Are certain times of day better for travel?

Approaching the checkpoint

- What is happening at the checkpoint?
  - Are vehicles being stopped?
  - Is there any problem or sign of violence?
  - Do the guards appear to be drunk?
- Is anything unusual about the checkpoint?
- Is it safe to turn back?

At the checkpoint

- If in doubt STOP, it is better to be told to move on than to be shot for not stopping!
- Have paperwork/documents ready
- The driver will normally talk to guards so make sure that they know what to say about you, your organisation and the purpose of your journey?
- Answer questions honestly
- While the driver is talking, passengers should remain quiet, respectful and alert – even if you do not understand the language that is being spoken

After the checkpoint

If appropriate:

- Report that you are through the checkpoint
- Report any incidents
- Consider changing your route for the return journey

DRIVING IN CONVOY

Driving in convoy requires planning and organisation. Drivers should be trained in convoy skills and the convoy leader should brief everybody.

Briefing (e.g.):

- Purpose of the trip
- Number of passengers
- Route to be taken
- Communication procedures
- Any key personnel
    - E.g. VIPs, medics, vulnerable people, etc.
- Actions on:
    - Over-taking other vehicles
    - Checkpoints
    - Vehicles being separated
    - Arriving at destination
    - Breakdown
    - Ambush
    - Accident

Travelling in a convoy can be very tedious for the driver. As a passenger, it is your job to help them stay focussed; engage them in conversation, and stay alert yourself.

Drivers often make the mistake of trying to keep up with vehicles in the convoy by rushing to overtake other traffic. They must be assured that the convoy will not leave them behind if they take their time.

ARMOURED VEHICLES

Mine Resistant Ambush Protected (M.R.A.P.) Vehicles:

Without proper training, being in an armoured vehicle has its own problems. Not all so-called armoured vehicles provide proper protection. They should conform to a recognised standard and not be modified.

Advantages

- Hardens the target
- Gives protection against small arms
- Can be made to look like normal vehicles
- Occupants may survive a bomb blasts or I.E.D.

Disadvantages

- Drivers and passengers must be trained
- Occupants feel safer than they really are
- M.R.A.P. vehicles are less manoeuvrable
- Reduced off-road handling
- Passengers may find doors hard to open/close
- Occupants are still vulnerable to attack by rocket fire and other explosive devices
- Reduced interior space
- In the event of an accident, it can be hard for rescuers to access injured passengers

If using M.R.A.P. vehicles, do not overlook alternative security strategies due to the false sense of security that this may bring.

CRIME

Tips for avoiding crime

Sexual aggression

Civil unrest

Active shooter incidents

Interviews & meetings

Information security

Avoiding surveillance

Car-jack

Gifts, bribes & extortion

Abduction & kidnap

TIPS FOR AVOIDING CRIME

Have good information

- Ask around to find out what the potential dangers are in your locality.
  - Where do the locals avoid?
  - What are the common types of crime?
  - Who is being targeted?

Preparation

- Think ahead and know where you are going
- Choose a safe route to get to your destination

Remain alert

- Get into the habit of 'seeing' what is around you
  - Is the area becoming more threatening?
  - What are other people doing?
  - Who is near to or following you?

Be unpredictable in your movements

- Change the routes you follow
- leave and return at different times

Trust your instincts

- If a place just feels wrong, leave immediately – you can work out why later on.

Don't get lazy...

- ...but don't be paranoid either

SEXUAL AGGRESSION

Sexual aggression includes any unwanted sexual act or suggestion. In many parts of the world, little support is given to victims of sexual violence – sometimes quite the opposite. Prosecution of offenders is rare. In all cases, care of the victim must be the first priority.

Definitions
Sexual harassment

- Unwanted suggestions/advances of a sexual nature

Sexual Assault

- Unwanted physical contact of a sexual nature

Rape

- Unwanted penetration

Avoiding harassment

- Do not be naïve – be careful about the messages you give to people regarding your feelings towards them
- Across cultures, there is variation about what different behaviours mean and expectations about people's behaviour – be clear about what you mean
- Travel can be a lonely activity, see loneliness for what it is and do not put yourself at risk just for the sake of some company
- If you receive unwanted advances, the sooner you make it clear that you are not interested, the easier it usually is to deal with the problem

Responding to an attack

If you are attacked, your main aim must be to survive. You have 3 options:

Submit to the attack

- If you choose to acquiesce, this is NOT giving consent and what happens to you is not your fault – it does not make it right or legal
- You might choose to submit if you feel it is too dangerous to do anything else or are unable to resist

Passively resist

- try to persuade the attacker to stop
- try to shame the attacker into stopping
- Make yourself less desirable (e.g. urinate, defecate)
- Ask the attacker to wear a condom

Actively resist – fight, scream, etc.

- This may be the only option if your life is in danger
- Be aware that fighting back may worsen the attack

Immediate care for a victim

- Who does the victim want to be with?
- Know your limitations – if you witnessed the assault, you may need support as well
- Avoid imposing your views or opinions on the victim
- Do they need immediate medical care for
  - Injuries
  - Advice on HIV prophylaxis
  - Psychological distress

Reporting sexual violence

Be aware of the issues around reporting sexual violence to local authorities, reactions will vary depending upon which part of the world you are in. In some places, the victim of an attack may find themselves accused of other crimes such as homosexuality or prostitution. This is unfair but unfortunately it is a reality that you should be aware of before deciding whether or not to report an attack.

Organisational responsibilities

Organisations whose staff may be exposed to sexual violence must have procedures in place for dealing with such an event before it actually happens. Making things up ad hoc is not acceptable and would be ignoring the duty of care that the organisation has towards its staff.

Confidentiality is important

- What are the reporting procedures?
  - Who should know?
  - Who does not need to/or should not know?
  - What will other staff be told?
  - How will personal information be kept secure?
- What care will be provided for the victim and their colleagues, friends, relatives?
- Who will provide this care - both medical and psychological?

The psychological impact of an attack may not affect the victim immediately. Organisations should consider how they support the longer-term welfare of the victim.

If you are a victim of a sexual assault

Individual responses to attacks vary from person to person. Some people cope well, others less so. The affects may be immediate or may only become apparent much later on (weeks, months or even years).

If you have been a victim of sexual violence, directly or indirectly, it is important to remember that you are not in any way to blame and that you do not deserve to suffer as a consequence – seek help that is appropriate to your needs.

Sexual aggression can be a problem for many travellers and is worsened by factors such as being away from family and friends, having to deal with unfamiliar authorities (if you choose to report the attack) and sometimes less than adequate medical support.

If you are travelling to an area where you think that sexual aggression might be a problem, think carefully about whether you are prepared to put yourself at risk, get more information and find out what the procedures would be if a problem did occur.

It is also worth remembering that colleagues that you travel with may not always be trustworthy. Be careful about any 'messages' you project in terms of availability and affection and be careful when you are socialising not to be completely unguarded.

Protests and riots can break out for many reasons and in response to both local and international events. There will often be signs of increasing tension prior to a protest but sometimes they appear to happen spontaneously.

Avoidance

- Take warnings from any authorities seriously
- Stay up to date with news reports
- Listen to 'the word on the street'
- Be prepared to change your plans to avoid danger

If you encounter a protest or riot

If in a vehicle:

- Turn around and drive away, but be very careful not to injure any protesters or the mob will turn on you
- Lock the doors and stay in the vehicle if safe to do so

If on foot

- Try to merge with the crowd (blend in)
- Move to a side street – most protests move down a single route and roads either side may be empty
- Avoid constrictions where the crowd gets squeezed into a narrow area making it hard to move
- Identify yourself as someone who is not a threat
- Act passively and do not become confrontational
- Seek a safe building, e.g. embassy, church or other 'friendly' premises

ACTIVE SHOOTER INCIDENTS

If you hear shooting

- Stay inside and lock doors
- Do NOT go to windows/doors to see where the shooting is coming from
- Move away from the noise
- Do not go and look for the source of the gunfire
- Celebratory gunfire kills many people by accident each year – stay away from such situations

If you come under direct fire

If you are caught in an active shooter incident, take cover, observe and then *make a decision* as to what to do; you cannot afford to panic or freeze.

Take cover

- stop, drop, crawl

Observe

- Where is the danger
- What is happening around you
- Where can you escape to or hide

Act:

- RUN: Get away if you can
- HIDE: Seek shelter but remain alert
- FIGHT: As a last option

If you are fleeing danger

- Run for short bursts (2-3 seconds)
- Run individually and intermittently, not as one group
- Avoid light backgrounds that will expose your silhouette, stay in the shadows
- 'Roll' across walls and other barriers rather than climbing on top of them
- If you must look, look around (to the side of objects) and NOT over the top of them

Make a decision & do it

If you get away...

Stay away and do not return to the area until the authorities tell you it is safe to do so.

If you hide...

You may have to remain hidden for a long time. Remain alert and look for better shelter or opportunities to escape

Be aware that attackers sometimes pretend to be rescuers and call for people to show themselves.

If you fight...

This is your last option, use as much force as you need to, get others to help you.

INTERVIEWS & MEETINGS

If you are meeting people that you do not know or trust, you may want to consider some of the following questions when deciding if a meeting is safe to go to:

- Who requested the meeting and why?
- Who decided where the meeting would be?
  - Why did they choose this place?
  - Why did they choose this time?
- Do you know if anyone else will be at the meeting?
- Is the venue easily accessible?
  - Public places are usually safest
- Will you be going on your own?
- Can you take a colleague with you?
- Can a friend discretely watch the meeting and keep an eye out for your safety?
- Can somebody wait nearby for you?
- What is the route to the meeting place?
- Arrange for someone to call you during the meeting to check that you are okay? Have a code word to use if you need help as you may not be able to talk freely if there is a problem
- Can you check out the venue before the meeting?
- How will you protect any sensitive information both during the meeting and while travelling?

When a meeting starts, let the other person know that "*I have to leave in 30 minutes as someone is expecting me*", you can always change your 'plans' if things are going well.

INFORMATION SECURITY

When travelling, do not take any information that you do not need (e.g. spare credit cards) and make backups of what you do take.

Photocopy the photo page of your passport and laminate the copy - use this as an identity card, but always have your full passport with you.

How information may be lost

Stealing

- Opportunistic or deliberate theft

Copying

- Photographing, downloading, copying, recording

Receiving

- Buying, extorting
- Eliciting (i.e. without the victim being aware that they have given information away)

General precautions

- Take only the information you will need
- Consider who is at risk if information is stolen, e.g. yourself, your clients, your family?
- Email important documents to avoid carrying them

In many countries, authorities can demand that you show them what is stored on your computer, smart phone, notepad, etc. Do not store any files that may arouse suspicion

Information technology

Unfortunately, the only sure way to avoid losing important data is to assume that your device will be stolen/hacked/copied and not keep anything important stored on it. Failing that, don't make it easy for the opportunistic or low-tech spy.

- Assume that information on a device will be stolen
- Be aware that it is not necessary to download any files for a computer to become infected with a virus
- Disable GPS/location tracking on phones
- Disable location settings on social media
- Do not share devices, including flash drives and memory sticks
- Assume that Wi-Fi connections are insecure
- Erase browsing history after using the internet, etc.
- In extreme cases, cameras and microphones on mobile phones may be turned on by hackers
- Assume any public IT service is monitored
- Review access logs for unaccounted logins, etc.
- Clear all data from devices before travel
- Encrypt files and email them to a secure address
- Update spyware, anti-virus and malware
- Disable scripting in browsers
- Do not open unknown emails or attachments
- Delete emails and erase phone messages immediately after reading/hearing
- Frequently reformat flash drives

AVOIDING SURVEILLANCE

There are many reasons why state forces may want to know about a traveller: suspicion of spying, to get you to spy for them or because you have contact with people they want to know more about. Similarly, business travellers may be victims of attempts by competitors to gain confidential product information. Do not be paranoid, but do be sensible about what you do and say.

Avoidance

- Do not behave suspiciously
- Be unpredictable by varying travel routes, times of departure and arrival, etc.
- Delete phone logs of recent calls and texts
- Assume that any IT devices are insecure
- Have a spare SIM card for making emergency calls only – Dispose of once used
- Arrange to meet people in public places
- Change vehicles
- Send decoy vehicles and people
- Keep your paperwork in order
    - E.g. passport, visas, permits to travel, etc.
- Encrypt and email important information and once read, securely delete from sent mail folders
- Regularly open new email accounts
- While away, use a different email account to your normal one and never email to the latter

CAR-JACK

In most cases of car-jacking, the perpetrators want the vehicle not the passengers. Your life is your most important possession, if stopped, do not get in the way of the car-jacker getting what they want.

Prevention

- Driver Training
- Keep travel to only necessary journeys
- Vary routes and travel times
- Need-to-know only sharing of travel plans
- Change travel plans at the last minute
    - E.g. departure time, route choice, destination

Car-jack tactics

- Holding-up stopped vehicles
- Roadblocks
- Fake accidents
- Bumping your vehicle
- Pedestrians pointing at a 'problem' with vehicle

Avoidance

- Low profile vehicles, or...
- ...Distinctive vehicles if this could help
- Keep vehicles moving at traffic lights, junctions, etc.
- Call ahead to have gates opened at compounds, etc.
- Remain alert while travelling
- Avoid car jack hotspots

If you are stopped

- Stay calm
- No sudden moves
- Take care when removing seatbelts and opening doors as the assailant might think that you are reaching for a weapon.
- Clearly indicate what you are doing
- Do as instructed by the car-jackers
- If told to lie down, avoid the back/front of vehicle
- Once the car-jackers are gone – get to safety fast

Once you have been stopped the best option is to acquiesce to the demands of the car-jackers. They will be aggressive and nervous; they want to get your vehicle and escape quickly...let them do it.

Occasionally, car-jackers will take victims with them for a short while (even to pay for fuel!), if this happens, remain calm and do as you are told. Do not stare at the car-jackers or do anything else to annoy or threaten them.

GIFTS, BRIBES & EXTORTION

Unlawfully or dishonestly paying money or offering gifts to get what you want is bribery. In many countries to pay a bribe is illegal. However, handing over valuables (including money) because someone is threatening you, is not paying a bribe, it is extortion.

Gifts

Before offering anyone a gift, as well as making sure it is appropriate, consider whether it could be misunderstood to be a bribe.

Paying bribes

Before you pay a bribe, think about the consequences

- Pay once and you will be expected to pay again
- Your colleagues will now be targeted for bribes
- It may be an attempt at entrapment
- You may end up in jail

In some countries, it is against the law for citizens to pay a bribe, no matter where in the world they happen to be

Resisting requests for money or gifts

If it is safe to do so, you could try to:

- Act like you think they are joking and smile
- Refuse or ask for a receipt
- Ask to speak to a more senior official
- Plead hardship or state that it is you and not your organisation that will have to pay

ABDUCTION & KIDNAP

Abduction is on the increase around the world and should be seen as a serious threat if you are travelling to a high risk area. Most abductions are planned, if you can understand how the perpetrators operate, you can take steps to avoid being the next victim.

In the event that someone is abducted, it is important to raise the alarm quickly as it may be possible to intervene before they are moved away from the immediate area.

Awareness

Who

- Which gangs are responsible?
- Are you likely to be a target?

Why

- What are the motives of the group?
- How do you fit in to their objectives?

How

- What methods are used, e.g. fake road blocks?

Where

- Offices, places of residence, on the street, etc.?

When

- At night/day time, leaving work, after festivals, etc.?

Avoiding abduction

Continually assess the level of risk and be prepared to change your plans

- Vary routines in order to be unpredictable
- Avoid working or travelling alone
- Disassociate from target groups
- Have a 'buddy system': A friend/colleague who will look out for you and call you if you do not turn up at work/at a party or do not return to your home/hotel, etc. You can do the same for them.

Stages of abduction

At the time of abduction, captivity, release and/or rescue, your objective is **SURVIVE!**

Capture

Capture is likely to be violent, comply with the abductors to reduce the chance of being injured

- Do NOT resist unless you are likely to be killed, remember:
  - Most kidnap victims will be freed
- Try to talk your way out, e.g.
  - *"My government does not pay ransom"*
  - *"Does your god want you to do this?"*
- Alert someone
  - Action must be taken to secure your release before the abductors sell you on to a more ruthless gang

Captivity

Decide to survive and get on with doing it. The experience is likely to be worse than anything you have imagined but the sooner you can start to adjust and be resolved to get through it, the better you will cope. Awful things may happen to you but unless you survive nobody can help you afterwards.

- Establish routines (mental and physical)
- Make yourself appear 'human' to your captors
  - E.g. talk about family, find common interests
- Ask for what you need
  - You may be able to get things to help you remain healthy and keep your mind occupied
- Argue calmly for your released
- Do not make any promises - leave this to the negotiators on the outside

Escape..!

Do NOT try to escape unless your life is in danger as you may make things worse for yourself if you are recaptured, and for any other people being held:

- Do you know where you are being held?
- Do you know where to go to find safety?
- What will happen to those you leave behind?
- What will happen if you are re-captured?

While escape may seem like a good idea, it is usually going to be much harder than it appears and the consequences of a failed attempt may be very bad.

Release

Over 80% of kidnap victims are released

- Expect many false releases - victims may be told they will soon be freed in order to keep them calm
- Remain alert during the release phase, observe and be ready to comply, run, hide or fight
- Do not relax until you are free and safely with people who will look after you
- Stay mentally strong until it is safe to let go

Rescue

Rescuers are there to subdue and if necessary kill the perpetrators as well as secure your freedom. An attempted rescue will be dangerous.

- Do NOT run towards your rescuers – they may shoot!
- Lie down, cover your head and keep your hands visible
- Identify yourself when the rescuers arrive
- Be prepared to run, hide or fight if your captors come to kill you
- Do exactly as the rescuers tell you

Rescuers are their to extract you to safety, not to give you hugs. Your hands may be tied and your your movements controlled.

- Comply with your rescuers, you will soon be given over to another team who will care for you

HOSTILE ENVIRONMENTS & WEAPONS OF WAR

Surviving hostile environments

Small arms fire

Ambush & crossfire

Roadside bombs

Bomb blasts

Grenade attack

Improvised explosive devices

Explosive remnants of war

Landmines

Cluster bombs

SURVIVING HOSTILE ENVIRONMENTS

If you are travelling in or near to a hostile environment then you probably already have an unusual attitude to risk. The most important thing to remember is that it's too late to regret taking chances if you're dead! Be prepared to change your plans if the situation worsens – avoid pushing on just because you can...

Intelligence/situational awareness

- Where is the danger coming from
- Who are the targets?
- Where are the hotspots?
- Who in your team can be trusted!

Avoid hotspots

- Stay away from military installations, convoys and other likely targets of attack

Robust communication systems

Use effective communication procedures and make sure your security people know

- Who you are
- Where you are
- Where you are going
- When you expect to arrive/return

First aid & medical provision

- Who has first aid skills, where is the medical care?

SMALL ARMS FIRE

Small arms and light weapons (SALW) are easily carried. Examples include pistols, rifles and grenade launchers. SALWs include both guns and weapons capable firing missiles and normally represent the most prevalent threat in a hostile environment.

Weapon range

Professional soldiers will usually refer to the effective range of a weapon, you should be more concerned about the killing range...

Effective range

- Useful range of the weapon for a trained professional in a combat situation

Killing range

- Distance at which a round from the weapon could kill

Examples

- Pistols
  - Effective range = about 10 to 15 metres
  - Killing range = about 50 to 100 metres
- Assault Rifles (e.g. AK47, M16)
  - Effective range = about 300 metres
  - Killing range = about 1000 to 1500 metres

NB: Celebratory gunfire (up into the air) kills many people each year – what goes up, really does come down. Take cover if you are nearby.

AMBUSH & CROSSFIRE

If your vehicle is moving

- Never stop in the killing zone
  - i.e. where the bullets are!
- Drive forward fast
  - If this is not possible, reverse fast
- Do NOT stop even if someone is injured
  - Passengers can administer first aid while moving
  - Stop when you are sure it is safe and check everybody for injuries

If you are immobilized

- Get away from the vehicle
  - Vehicles attract gunfire as they are obvious and large targets
  - Vehicles do NOT protect you from bullets
- The engine block may provide limited cover
- Be aware, someone may take the vehicle away
- Get to better cover
  - E.g. buildings, ditches, dead ground
  - Do not lie in ditches if the area is mined

Avoidance

- Know where attacks take place
- Avoid military convoys and other potential targets
- Only undertake essential journeys
- Vary your routes and journey times
- Travel only in daylight

ROADSIDE BOMBS

Roadside bombs can cause massive explosions and have a devastating affect on their target. Explosives may be hidden in drains, ditches, pipes and culverts. Hard top roads give some protection but cannot be assumed to be safe.

Avoidance

Understand who is likely to be a target and what, if any, are the patterns of attack. Also be aware of where previous attacks have occurred

- Be unpredictable with your travel schedule
- Vary your routes and journey times
- Share your itinerary only on a 'need to know' basis and consider changing the plan at the last minute
- Avoid military convoys or other likely targets
- If you are caught up with a military convoy
  - Pull over and let it pass
  - Wait 30 minutes or more before continuing
- Try to travel only on hard top road surfaces
- Avoid being the first vehicle to travel along a road on any given day – delay departure if necessary
- Check the security situation just before you depart
- Do not hesitate to change your plans and cancel your journey if the security signs are not good
- If you are in a danger area, do not become lazy just because nothing has happened for a while

BOMB BLASTS

Bomb blasts may be from traditional armaments or improvised devices, the latter being more commonly used outside the conventional battlefield area hence their use for spreading terror among civilian populations.

The severity of injury depends largely upon how close the victim is to the explosion. Multiple injuries to a casualty are common and a thorough examination needs to be made of the entire person to ensure that nothing is missed

Actions:

- Take Cover
- Drop to the Floor
- Cover your head
- Stay alert
  - You may lose your hearing (temporarily)
- Use emergency exits
- Move away from buildings
- Avoid crowds that gather at the scene as these may become the target of a second attack
- LEAVE THE AREA
  - You cannot help others if you get injured
  - Do not return until sure it is safe to do so

If you have been in or near to an explosion, it is important to get a full medical assessment as the effects may not be immediately apparent.

GRENADE ATTACK

How long till it explodes?

Grenades have a timed detonation but the attacker may delay releasing for several seconds. It is not possible to know how long it will be before the weapon detonates. Do NOT attempt to pick up or kick the grenade away as this may be the last thing you do.

Range of explosion:

- Effective Range: > 10 metres
- Killing Range: > 50 metres

Immediate action:

The blast from a grenade is often deflected upwards, therefore, if you can quickly get down to the floor you may avoid injury

- Shout "GRENADE!" while you...
    1. Take one step and dive away
    2. Cross legs
    3. Open mouth
    4. Cover head/ears

After an attack, move quickly to shelter and be alert for other devices coming towards you.

If you are vulnerable to grenade attack, practice, practice, practice your grenade drill.

IMPROVISED EXPLOSIVE DEVICES

Improvised explosive devices (I.E.D.s) are a favoured weapon of the terrorist. Often deployed outside of the conventional field of combat, they may be placed in offices, public places, religious sites, etc. I.E.D.s may be any size, intricate or simple, stable or unstable. Some are detonated by the victim, others by remote control.

If you suspect there is an I.E.D., get out of the area and take others with you. Raise the alarm but do not use your phone until away from the suspect device.

Types of I.E.D.

- BBIED – 'Body borne IED'/Suicide Bomber
- VBIED – 'Vehicle borne IED'
- UVIED – 'Under vehicle IED'
- Roadside IED
- Booby Traps

Avoidance

- Get information and training
- What are the motives of the attackers
- Who are the targets
- Types of attack
- Be careful of 'interesting' /valuable objects that are out of place (e.g. cigarettes, toys, phones, TVs, etc.)
- If possible, avoid any location where attacks have occurred in the past

EXPLOSIVE REMNANTS OF WAR

Explosive Remnants of War (ERW) present a significant hazard to anyone travelling in an area within or around an existing or previous conflict zone.

Explosive munitions remain hazardous for many years, even centuries, after they have been lost or abandoned. Estimates suggest that more than 80 countries are significantly affected by these artefacts.

Categories of ERW

Unexploded Ordnance (UXO)

This term refers to explosive munitions that have been used but for some reason failed to detonate. It is estimated that as much as 30% of explosive weaponry fails to detonate and so UXO are very common.

Abandoned Ordnance

During and after a conflict, stores of munitions may be abandoned or simply forgotten. These caches may be large or small and it is difficult to predict where they will be found.

Examples of ERW

E.R.W. include an array of explosive weaponry, e.g. cluster bombs, mortar shells, artillery shells, rockets, bullets, bombs, fuses and detonators, etc.

Awareness & avoidance

All ERW is assumed to be unstable/unsafe

In or near to areas of conflict:

- Treat any unidentified objects with caution
- Do not touch anything you cannot positively identify
- Be aware of anything with an aerodynamic shape and/or 'military' colouring
- Materials include plastic and/or metal
    - But items may become rusty and dirty
- Missile propellant can cause injury too
- Size may vary from centimetres to several metres
    - E.g. grenades to anti aircraft missiles
- Look out for signs of packaging that may indicate the presence of ERW – boxes, papers, etc.
- Fuses and detonators, although often small, contain very high explosives and come in a variety of shapes and sizes. They may have springs or pins attached

Location of ERW:

- Anywhere in or near an existing or historical combat area or military installation, and...
    - Buildings and building remains, rooftops, cellars
    - Compound grounds
    - Trees, hedges, rivers and other natural features
    - Under, on and above ground level
- Do not assume that civilian areas will be safe

ERW's do not make good souvenirs and people have been arrested trying to take them home!

LANDMINES

Besides small arms, landmines are one of the commonest causes of injury to civilians by conventional weaponry. The danger is enhanced by the difficulty in knowing exactly where they are, their indiscriminate nature and their persistence long after a conflict has ceased.

Types of landmine
Anti-personnel mines

Designed to kill or injure individual people

- **Blast mines** – the force of the explosion directly causes injury
- **Fragmentation mines** – flying shrapnel causes injury

Anti-vehicle mines

- Designed to disable tanks and heavily armoured vehicles.
- Will destroy light transport, including wagons, trucks and 4-wheel drive vehicles

Where found (e.g.)

- Near active and disused military installations
- Near high value infrastructure
  - E.g. power stations, pylons, airfields, factories
- Roadsides and open areas
- Sites where soldiers may rest
  - E.g. shade, warehouses, sources of water
- In or near to a former combat zone

Indications

Formal

- Signage
  - often triangular with skull and crossbones
- Hazard tape
  - with or without the word 'mine' written on it
- Red and white stones or sticks marking the perimeters of minefields or safe pathways and/or individual mines

Informal

- Varies depending on local custom
  - E.g. sticks with bottles on, crossed sticks, piles of stones, knotted grass

Other Indications

- Presence of amputees in local communities
- Dead cattle and unharvested crops where none would be expected – e.g. where people are hungry
- Odd bits of wire and metal lying on the ground
- Tracks that avoid obvious/shorter routes
- Patches of disturbed ground

Sources of information

- Local Mine Action Groups (M.A.G.'s)
- Military
- UN de-mining agency
- Local people - but assume their knowledge is limited

Landmines & vehicles

If mines are known to be in the area

- Stay on hard top roads
- Never drive over anything
- Do not drive off the road to avoid an object
- Stay in the wheel tracks of other vehicles – this may be difficult if driving a wide vehicle

Actions on being in a minefield

- STOP
- Warn others
- Standstill/do not drive out
- Wait for help
- (Self-extraction is not an option)

Landmine facts

- A single person can detonate a vehicle mine
- It is not safe to probe for mines with a stick
- Mines float and rain may cause them to creep out of cordoned off areas
- Vehicle mines will often be found among anti-personnel mines to destroy de-mining machinery
- It is impossible to safely re-trace your steps in a minefield - the foot pressure will change even if the print is the same
- Walking along your vehicle's tracks to escape a minefield does not guarantee safety - your vehicle may have already disturbed a mine

CLUSTER BOMBS

Cluster bombs are usually dropped from the air, the bomb then disperses large numbers of bomblets over a wide area.

Bomblets can land anywhere and commonly get hung up in trees and on roof-tops. They remain active for many years and cause many casualties among civilians, particularly children who may be attracted to these curious objects.

Background

- Each bomb may contain as many as 800 bomblets
- Estimates suggest that 30% of cluster bombs fail to explode
- Soft ground may be a cause of failure to detonate

Signs

- Small parachutes lying around
- Destroyed foliage and other signs of small explosions
- 'Splash' signs on roads and buildings where bomblets have detonated

Avoidance

- See 'Explosive Remnants of War'

FIELD FIRST AID

Incident management

First aid essentials

Casualty report

Altitude sickness

Diarrhoea

Stress

Tear gas/water cannon

Malaria

Cross contamination

INCIDENT MANAGEMENT

Fundamental to managing the immediate consequences of an incident is the need for leadership, a plan and a decision to act. In a group situation, the senior person is not always the most able when it comes to coping with an incident.

Principles

Every incident requires leadership to:

- Coordinate resources
- See the bigger picture
- Keep others informed

In a first aid emergency

You may not be able to save everyone – so help those that you can

Order of treatment:

1. Those who can't wait/need immediate help
2. Those who can wait but will get worse
3. The 'walking wounded'
4. Those who are likely to be beyond help

Evacuation:

The priorities for evacuation may not be the same as for treatment and should be assessed separately.

- Evaluate - Treat - Evaluate – Evacuate
- Consider the implications of evacuating and have a contingency plan in case of difficulties

FIRST AID ESSENTIALS

In the event of a person being injured or taken ill, follow this procedure:

Primary Check

Check for Danger

- Is it safe, remember, you are no good to anyone if you get injured too!
  - Is there a threat from other people?
  - Are vehicles leaking fuel?
  - Are there any sharp objects/broken glass?
  - In a bomb attack, could there be another device?

Check & Stop Catastrophic bleeding

- I.e. any bleeding that is so bad the casualty will die if you do not stop it immediately (but try to check and open the airway while you do this)

Check for Alertness

- Is the victim awake and aware of all that is happening to them or are they unconscious?

Airway

- Is the victim's airway open?
- Gently tilt the head back and pull the chin forward

Breathing

- Is the casualty breathing normally?

Circulation

- Are there any other signs of bleeding?
  - Check all over: look and feel, move the clothing, cut and remove clothing

Secondary Check

Examine the casualty from head to toe:

- Compare one side with the other
- Shape, size, colour, temperature

Head:

- Bumps or depressions in the skull
- Bleeding from ears/nose
- Damage to face, blueness to lips

Neck & Shoulders:

- Deviation of windpipe
- Raised veins on the neck
- Swelling or puffiness
- Symmetry and stability of shoulders/collarbone

Chest:

- Bi-lateral, smooth, regular breathing
- Sucking sounds/penetrating wounds
- Uneven, asymmetrical breathing

Abdomen:

- Tension, swelling, bruising
- Penetrating wounds, exposed intestines

Pelvis:

- Injuries can be very unstable – do not move unnecessarily
- Visually check for symmetry
- Soiling or wetting

Legs & Arms

- Compare and check for deformity, swelling and tenderness

Recovery/Safe Airway Position

If the casualty is unconscious:

- Put them on their side so that fluid can drain from the mouth
- Ensure the airway is open
- Keep checking their breathing

Get help

- Do not forget to call for help!

Mind what you say

- Always talk to a victim
- Even if they are unconscious, they may be able to hear you

Missed bleeds

- Failure to find a missed bleed, is a major cause of avoidable death in first aid – keep looking!

After finding & treating injuries:
Decide

- Little sick – I can deal with this
- Big Sick – I need help

Getting help

If there is no paramedic service, options may be to evacuate the casualty yourself or to bring help to the casualty.

CASUALTY REPORT - A.T.M.I.S.T.

A	**Age, Name, Sex** Get the casualties details quickly in case they become unconscious
T	**Time** Time of the incident... ...or time that you arrived at the scene Be clear which of these you have recorded
M	**Mechanism of Injury** What happened to cause the injuries? E.g. *"Casualty was knocked off a motorbike"*
I	**Injuries** Describe what you see, not what you think is wrong – unless you're qualified to do so
S	**Signs & Symptoms** What is the casualty telling you What can you see or measure (temperature, pulse, breathing rate, colour, consciousness)
T	**Treatment Given/Needed** What have you done What do you plan to do What help do you need

ALTITUDE SICKNESS

Altitude sickness can affect anyone travelling to over 2500 metres above sea level. Delays in identifying and treating altitude sickness are a common cause of death and diagnosis can be delayed by the fact that the victim may not be aware that they are ill.

Avoidance

- Ascend slowly
- Take regular rest days
- Avoid over exerting yourself
- Drink plenty of non-alcoholic fluids

If you are unlucky, you may still get sick! Most people show temporary, *mild* signs as they ascend to altitude

Lake Louise Assessment System

	0	1	2	3
Headaches	None	Mild	Moderate	Severe
Appetite loss/nausea	None	Mild	Moderate	Severe
Tiredness/fatigue	None	Mild	Moderate	Severe
Dizziness	None	Mild	Moderate	Severe
Sleeping Habit	Good	Not good	Poor	Very poor

Score 3-5: do not ascend until recovered

Score more than 5: descend immediately

DIARRHOEA

Stomach upsets can be mild or severe and many people treat them as an inevitable part of travelling, this is not true. Good habits will prevent most cases of diarrhoea.

Avoidance:

- Good hygiene habits
  - wash hands before eating
  - avoid putting fingers in your mouth
- Eat only cooked food or peeled fruit and vegetables
- Wash fruit and vegetables in drinking water
- Use bottled water and make sure the lid is secure before opening a new bottle

Even if you think the tap-water is 'probably' OK, is it worth risking your trip to find out?

Treatment:

Give sugars and salts with plenty of liquid. Proprietary re-hydration powders are OK but you can also use a Litre of drinking water with 2-4 teaspoons of sugar, ½ teaspoon of salt and a pinch of bicarbonate of soda.

Be aware:

Most cases of diarrhoea pass in 24-48 hours but sometimes they indicate more serious illness such as cholera, typhoid and hepatitis A. If in doubt as to what is causing the problem or you are not recovering, seek medical help.

STRESS

Stress can be understood as a reaction to an event or circumstance that negatively affects the person's mental and/or physical well-being.

Stress and distress can be caused by a single 'critical event' - a situation so removed from ones normal experience that it is hard to cope with, examples include being a witness to a violent attack or being attacked yourself. Or it may be that stress is due to long term exposure to a challenging situation such as being away from family and friends for long periods, persistent noise, bullying, etc.

No one is immune to stress but reactions to distressing circumstances vary from individual to individual. It is important to understand and recognise the personal signs of stress in yourself so that you can address them before they become a problem.

Some common signs of stress:

- Lack of ability to concentrate
- Poor sleep
- Loss of appetite
- Mood changes, e.g. withdrawal or anger
- Loss of motivation
- Increased alcohol consumption
- Excessive worrying
- Self-destructive behaviours

Managing stress

It is important to deal with stress before it becomes a significant problem in your life. The longer it continues the harder it can be to address the problem and a person may even become desensitized to the damage it is doing.

Things that can help include:

- Rest and a change of routine
- A change of activity
- Talking to friends
- Exercise
- A healthy diet
- Avoiding alcohol
- Keeping a sense of perspective

Post-Traumatic Stress Disorder (PTSD)

If a person has been exposed to a critical event it is normal to show signs of stress such as flashbacks, disrupted sleep, worrying about the event, etc. Usually, these problems recede and dissipate within 4-6 weeks. If a person continues to experience distress after this time, or the problem worsens, it is important to get help. PTSD is not uncommon and there is nothing weak or abnormal if you find yourself suffering and need to get help.

TEAR GAS/WATER CANNON

Chemicals used to disperse crowds cause intense irritation to the eyes, nasal passage and mouth. They can also cause difficulty in breathing especially if you have an existing problem such as asthma

Limiting the effects

- Do not wear contact lenses
- Avoid oil based lotions and creams (e.g. sun cream) that cause chemicals to stick to the skin
- Carry plenty of water to wash your face with
- Do not try to pick up a tear gas canister - it will be very hot and can burn skin
- Immediately move away from the area
- Try to get upwind of the gas if it is safe to do so

After contact

- Stand with your face into the wind if possible
- Wash with an alkaline based solution
  - E.g. bicarbonate of soda
  - Many antacid tablets can be used to make a solution
- Remove contaminated clothing before going indoors
- Place contaminated clothes straight into a plastic bag
- Take a shower and wash from the head down
- Be careful not to get chemicals onto other people

MALARIA

Malaria kills! Do not assume that you are safe just because other people are not protecting themselves from the risk of malaria.

Prevention – avoiding mosquito bites

- Apply insect repellent on skin paying attention around the wrists and ankles where bites are very common. A 50% solution DEET based repellent is best and has been tried and tested for years
- Insecticide – on clothing. Remember to refresh regularly as washing will reduce effectiveness
- Cover as much of the skin as is practicable
- Use a mosquito net at night and ensure that it is large enough to keep you fully covered
- Avoid going out when mosquitoes are most active such as after rain and in the evening

Prophylaxis

Anti-malarial medication protects you if you become infected. Many people do not like to take the medication because of misinformation and uncertainty around the side-effects. It is vital to take your anti-malarial tablets, speak to your doctor if your are unsure about anything.

Temporary 'Immunity' after infection cannot be relied upon. Continue to use prophylaxes. There are several types of malaria, a slight immunity to one will not protect your from the others.

CROSS CONTAMINATION

The risks

- A person who has an infectious disease does not have to be ill to infect someone else, however...
- ...Infection through normal contact is very unlikely in most cases

Causes

The principal cause of infection is exposure to blood and other body fluids caused by:

- Sexual activity
- Open wounds and damaged skin
- Wounds caused by infected instruments and sharp objects, e.g. needles, scalpels, broken glass

Prevention

- Follow good hygiene procedures
  - Washing of hands is one of the most effective ways to avoid cross contamination
- Avoid exposure to 'sharps' and if handling needles, make sure that you know how to do this safely
- Cover all breaks to the skin with waterproof dressing
- Carry and use suitable gloves
  - For administering first aid
  - When cleaning any body fluids
- Consider using a mask and goggles if appropriate
- Dispose of waste safely

In the event of exposure

- Wash the skin with soap and running water
- If you have been cut, encourage the wound to bleed
    - Do NOT suck the injury
- If splashed in the face, wash eyes, nose and mouth using tap water but do not swallow
- Seek medical advice quickly
- Treatment for infections may be more effective if administered rapidly

Exposure to HIV

Human immunodeficiency virus (HIV) causes the acquired immune deficiency syndrome (AIDS)

If you suspect that you may have been exposed to the HIV virus, prophylactic drugs are available that may help to prevent infection. These will have to be prescribed by a doctor and should be taken within 72 hours of infection, but the earlier the better.

These prophylactic drugs can cause severe side-effects and so professional after-care is essential. You may also need psychological counselling.

If exposure is considered a significant risk, an emergency response plan should be prepared.

SURVIVING NATURAL DISASTERS

Natural disasters

Emergency evacuation

Emergency shelter

Missing person card

NATURAL DISASTERS

If you are travelling to a region of the world that is known to be vulnerable to natural disasters it is important to consider what you will do in an emergency. Many people may be affected and you may have to look after yourself if the civil defence services are overstretched.

Often, natural disasters are predictable in that they are known to occur in specific regions of the world. As a result, authorities will normally have a civil defence system in place designed to advise, warn and protect the population from harm. If you are travelling in an area that is vulnerable to natural disasters, it is important that you find out what this system is and follow any advice given to you.

In the event of a natural disaster the emergency services will direct their attention to those in most need, communications and transport lines may be broken, food, clean water and shelter may be unavailable. You must be prepared to survive without assistance, possibly for several days.

It is useful to have a radio available so that you can listen to broadcasts from the authorities which may tell you where you can get help.

Earthquakes

If you are in an earthquake area, try to stay in places that are less vulnerable such as quake-proof buildings and away from possible landslides and floods

- If you are in a building during an earthquake it is usually too late or too difficult to get out
- Hide under doorways and other designated areas
- After the earthquake, be aware of other dangers such as unstable buildings, broken gas and electrical services

Typhoons/Hurricanes

If you are asked to evacuate an area before a storm arrives...do it. During the storm:

- Seek shelter but make sure that it is strong enough to resist the high winds.
- Avoid going outside as there will be flying that debris can cause injury
- Stay away from windows as they may break suddenly

Flooding

Never underestimate the power of moving water - a cubic metre of water weighs 1 tonne!

- Avoid going into water if at all possible - a long detour is better than drowning
- What will happen if you get swept away?
- Do not try to drive through deep water

EMERGENCY EVACUATION

Evacuating from a danger zone can be a high risk activity, it is important to evaluate all of your options and to consider what you will do if you cannot complete the evacuation successfully

When to evacuate?

As a general rule, if you are going to have to evacuate from danger, it is better to do this sooner rather than later when the situation may have become more difficult.

Deciding to evacuate:

- Assess all your options
- Set a clear objective and agree upon a plan
- Be sure you can get to your objective
- Think about what will happen if you get stuck or lost on the way
- Let potential rescuers know what your plan is and how you will stay in contact
- Make sure everyone understands what is going to happen by telling them the plan and asking them to repeat it back to you.
- Be careful not to underestimate the difficulty of your journey or overestimate the speed you will move at
- If you are carrying someone on a stretcher, you will need at least 6 people and to rest every 50 to 100 metres.
- It may be very slow going – be realistic

EMERGENCY SHELTER

It is easy to make an emergency shelter to protect yourself from the elements: rain, snow, wind and sun. Make your shelter before you are exhausted.

To make a shelter:

Choose a good location

- Out of the wind, dry and safe from flooding
- ...but make sure you can still be found by rescuers

Improvise

- Think about what you are trying to achieve rather than the objects you would like to have
  - E.g. rather than wishing you had a tent, think about materials that can keep out the weather

Prepare

- Make sure that the ground is suitable and flat
- Put down plastic, cardboard, carpet, etc., for insulation

Plan

Now you have a shelter consider your other needs

- Do you have adequate food and water?
- What other materials and resources are available?
- How will you keep warm?
- How will potential rescuers find you?
- Are you safe from other threats?

A tarpaulin shelter

- Get a piece of plastic, canvas, tarpaulin - any strong waterproof sheet - and some chord
- Anchor the corners securely
- Use the chord to make a ridge line that you can lie the tarpaulin over
- Stretch out the fabric so it does not flap around in the wind and tear itself to pieces
- Use trees, poles, etc. to get some height under the shelter and to ensure that water will run off
- Fasten the chord and/or tarpaulin to the ground using stakes, pegs, sticks, etc.
- If you need to collect water, place a bucket at the run off point

Simple shelters:

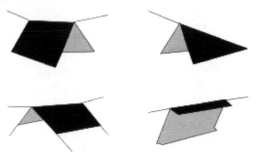

MISSING PERSON CARD

Instructions:

If you are involved in a large scale emergency, such as after an earthquake or tsunami, it can be difficult to find people and to know if they are safe.

Often, makeshift notice boards appear on the streets after a large scale emergency. People will use these to tell others that they are safe and to try and contact those they have lost.

Fill in the details on the following page and pin it on a notice board..

MISSING PERSON

Name:

From:　(Town)　(Country)

I AM LOOKING FOR:

Name 1:

(From)

Name 2:

(From)

Name 3:

(From)

I can be contacted at:

Telephone:

Email:

Location:

If you know where any of these people are,

please contact me.

Thank you.

COMMUNICATIONS

Communication hardware

Radio procedure

Common radio terms

Phonetic alphabet

Incident reporting

Global positioning systems

COMMUNICATION HARDWARE

A large variety of devices are available for communications ranging from the simple to the sophisticated. Each type of system has advantages and disadvantages.

Mobile phones

Advantages: readily available, easy to use, can store contacts and other information, two-way conversation simultaneously, networks are quite robust and quickly re-established after incidents.

Disadvantages: Can only contact one person at a time, authorities may block access in an emergency, not secure, cost of usage, often stolen.

Satellite phones

Advantages: Can operate almost anywhere, not dependent on a local network, some can send location data, getting cheaper each year, easy to use.

Disadvantages: Expensive, may attract unwanted attention (e.g. suspicion of spying), may be illegal without a permit in some countries, slow to boot up, poor reception without clear view of sky. Signal may be intermittent

Different satellite networks have different advantages and disadvantages, e.g. some are better for data and others for voice communications.

Two-way radios (HF & VHF)

For voice communications, very high frequency (VHF) and High Frequency (HF) radios are the most common devices. Most hand-held radios will be VHF, have a limited range and be limited to 'line-of-sight' communications. HF radios are capable of transmitting very long distances but require more skill to operate as it may be necessary to change frequencies regularly due to atmospheric conditions.

Advantages: Cheap to buy and limited running costs. It is possible to communicate with multiple people simultaneously and they are independent of any phone network which can be major advantages if there is a security alert. VHF radios are easy to maintain and use.

Disadvantages: Open channels mean that anyone can listen in on conversations. The range may be very limited with VHF radio but HF radio requires more knowledge to use effectively. It may be necessary to have a permit to operate the radio and signals can easily be jammed.

Tracking devices

Advantages: Provide accurate location data, can be set up to send automatic updates, can be used to signal an emergency, some can be used to send SMS messages, observers can monitor the users from the internet.

Disadvantages: Different technologies with varying limitations, cannot receive messages, may rely upon local phone network to send data.

RADIO PROCEDURE

If you are not familiar with using radios it can seem like you are learning a whole new way of communicating. However, the only objective is to be clearly understood and following a few simple procedures will help:

- Talk in a normal voice, but not too quickly
- Hold the radio a little way from your mouth otherwise it will not sound clear – (1-2"/2.5-5.0cm)
- Try to get out of the wind
- Listen before you speak
  - Is anybody using the channel already?
- Remember
  - You must press the button to talk...
  - ...and release the button to hear
- Do not talk until you have pressed the talk button
  - Press, wait 0.5 seconds, talk
- Keep each transmission short
  - Break long messages into several smaller parts
- Avoid using unnecessary code words unless absolutely necessary
- Listening to how others use the radio is a great way to learn the techniques
- Knowing a few common radio terms will help you to communicate efficiently

COMMON RADIO TERMS

Call sign

The unique name you use (e.g. '*Alpha One*')

Radio check

A routine check, normally daily, to ensure that radios are working and, in security situations, that the user is still okay.

Contact procedure

How to initiate and acknowledge a call, e.g.

- *"Base, base, base, this is alpha. Over."*
- *"base for alpha, go ahead. Over."*

Over

End of my sentence, it's your turn to speak

Out

I have nothing more to say

Say again

Pardon

Do you copy?/Copy that

Do you understand?/I understand

Standby

Wait a moment, but keep listening

Emergency, emergency, emergency

Use this *only* in an emergency

PHONETIC ALPHABET

It is useful to be able to spell uncommon words using the phonetic alphabet such as the one below. If you cannot remember a word choose another that begins with the same letter but make sure it will be clearly understood.

A	Alpha	M	Mike
B	Bravo	N	November
C	Charlie	O	Oscar
D	Delta	R	Romeo
E	Echo	S	Sierra
F	Foxtrot	T	Tango
G	Golf	U	Uniform
H	Hotel	V	Victor
I	Indigo	W	Whisky
J	Juliet	X	X-ray
K	Kilo	Y	Yankee
L	Lima	Z	Zulu

Figures

Numbers are easily misheard over radio so break them down into small chunks (e.g. "123456789" becomes "123 – 456 – 789") and ask the listener to repeat them back.

INCIDENT REPORTING

If reporting an incident, you are more likely to get the help you need if your information is clearly structured. Do not assume that the person on the other end of a radio or phone is a specialist, they may need to pass the information on to someone else.

Who

Say who you are/who is affected – use your call sign

Where

Location

When

Time of the incident

What

Describe what happened

What

Describe what you have done

What

Describe what you are going to do

What

Say what support you need

GLOBAL POSITIONING SYSTEMS (GPS)

Global Positioning Systems, commonly known as GPS, refer to networks of satellites and ground stations that transmit data that can be received by devices capable of using this information to calculate positions with high levels of accuracy.

Many devices now incorporate GPS functions but, unless the user is able to understand and interpret the information they provide, they may give the user a false sense of awareness.

To use the way-marking, tracking, routing and other functions of a GPS device it is important to understand some key concepts including:

Coordinate Reference Systems

- E.g. WGS84, UTM, longitude and latitude

Accuracy & Error

What is the accuracy and extent of any deviation? E.g. if a device is 95% accurate, what does that mean in practice? Is it accurate to 10, 20 or 50 metres and how far out could it be the other 5% of the time - up to 100m, up to a kilometre?

In short, if you have a GPS device, make sure you know how to use it and what the data is telling you.

APPENDIX

Developing a security strategy

Awareness

Security factors

Information & security

Understanding the security environment

Situational awareness

Actor mapping

Time lines

Putting it all together

Approaches to security

Risk management

Dangers, hazards & threats

Standard operating procedures

Contingency planning

AWARENESS

Safety & security begins with understanding the general context and then narrows to focus upon specific dangers. It is important to take a systematic approach.

General awareness

Culture, economics, history, politics...

Awareness of dangers

Health, crime, hostility...

Impact & exposure to dangers

Risk Assessment

Reduction of exposure & impact

Risk management

- Standard Operating Procedures
- Contingency Planning
- Escape and Evacuation Plans

Maintaining awareness

Vigilance: active awareness and re-assessment

F
O
C
U
S

SECURITY FACTORS

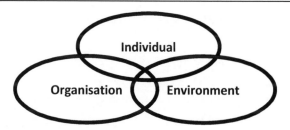

Individual Factors

- Experience
- Awareness
- Gender
- Age
- Ethnicity
- Attitude to risk
- Peer pressure
- Etc.

Organisation

- Awareness
- Support of senior management
- Training provision
- Up-to-date knowledge
- Security systems

Environment

- War
- Poverty
- Rule of law
- Remnants of war
- Geography
- Natural hazards
- Emergency services
- Etc.

INFORMATION & SECURITY

Sources of security information

Formal Sources

- Safety & security briefings
- Organisational documents
- Embassies, governments, security specialists
- Law enforcement agencies...

Informal Sources

- Other workers/travellers
- Websites (e.g. for local papers)
- Local people
- Hotel reception...

Triangulation

Gather information from several sources and look for the consistent themes

- Questions to ask of the information
  - Is it up-to-date, reliable, and relevant?
  - Who gathered the information and for what purpose?

Staying up to date

It is important to regularly review security. The immediate situation may change but international events may also have a direct or indirect affect on the level of threat in a given region.

UNDERSTANDING THE SECURITY ENVIRONMENT

Understanding the environment and culture in which you are working is the first stage in developing a risk management strategy. Safety measures can only be as good as the knowledge of the hazards faced.

The General Environment

History

- Has your own country been in conflict with the country your are travelling to or does it have a colonial or political past in the region that could affect how you will be perceived?
- Have there been any inter-ethnic or tribal conflicts that might impact on the current security situation?
- Do certain events regularly lead to protest, violence or disruption in a community?

Culture

- Are there any customs that you should be aware of to avoid causing offence to local people?

Law & Order

- Are there any specific laws that could affect you?

Socio-Economics

- What is the distribution of wealth in the country and where do you fit into this hierarchy?

SITUATIONAL AWARENESS

The Immediate Environment

Be aware of your immediate environment be it a building, a public place, on the road, at a bus or railway station, etc.

- Are there any immediate threats?
- What is going on around me?
- Where are the emergency exits?
- Who is near to me?
- Is anything unusual?
- Where is my vehicle?
- Are people avoiding me/my vehicle?
- Is anyone trying to distract me?
- What would I do right now if something happened?
- Can I see any approach routes clearly?
- Where are my personal belongings?
- Do I need to leave this place now?
- Who could help me?
- Where could I escape to?
- How would I get help if I needed it?

Situational awareness means being observant as you enter a new setting and staying alert to changes while you are there. If you make a conscious effort to be aware it will soon become second nature and not interfere with your other activities.

ACTOR MAPPING

Who's Who?

Who are the major authorities, organisations, and individuals in the area and how do your activities relate to each of them?

Mapping or drawing out the relations in a visual representation can be a very effective way of understanding how different actors and agents may affect your safety.

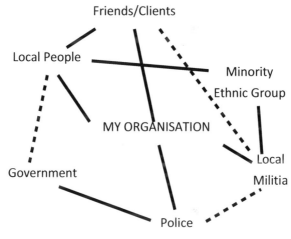

Key:

Good relations ──────

Poor relations ▬ ▬ ▬ ▬ ▬

Etc...

TIME LINES

Drawing historical and more contemporary time lines can help you understand the overall history and patterns of specific events...

Colonized by Britain	1860
Insurrection began	1905
Massacre of northern tribes	1910
Independence	1948
First elections	1949
Coup	1955
President killed	1970
Democratic elections	1982
Northern tribes rebel	1991
UN peace keeping mission	1998

PUTTING IT ALL TOGETHER

Context

- Understand the wider environment, culture, politics and socio-economic setting
- Understand the major safety & security threats
- Understand the specific safety & security issues that might affect you

Actor mapping

- Understand how different individuals and groups interact, including your own relationship with these elements
- Identify which relationships need developing and maintaining
- Identify which people and groups to avoid

Manage the risks

- Understand the specific threats and hazards you may encounter – direct and indirect
- Identify methods for reducing the risks you face (acceptance, protection, deterrence)
- Implement safety plans via standard operating procedures:
  - What you will do normally to remain safe?
- Establish contingency plans
  - What you will do in the event of an incident?

APPROACHES TO SECURITY

Approaches to security are often divided into 3 different strategies for making people and property less likely to be the deliberate target of an attack or crime: acceptance, protection and deterrence. Each strategy has its advantages and limitations. In reality, a comprehensive security system is likely to include elements from more than one of these areas:

Acceptance

Acceptance means gaining the trust of other people and groups so that we and/or our property are not targeted for attacks. In an ideal world, acceptance would always be the preferred method of staying safe and reducing threats. Acceptance can have the additional advantage that people look out for and warn us when there are potential threats to our safety.

An example of an acceptance strategy might be to meet with community elders and explain the purpose of your visit, research or work in the area, and the possible benefits to their community.

However, this approach is not always effective. Some groups may not respond to arguments or may divert their attacks on to other people.

Protection

The purpose of protection is to make the person or property a more challenging target, i.e. 'Hardening the target'. Examples of protection include the use of armoured vehicles, gated compounds, guards and other security procedures.

The main limitation of a protection strategy is that the threat itself is not removed (e.g. people may still want to kidnap you even though you have made it harder for them to do so), and protection can never be 100% effective.

A further limitation of this approach is that many of the techniques put barriers between those who are protected and the wider community. This can be a problem if your work requires cooperating or engaging with those outside of your immediate environment and be counter-productive to any acceptance strategy.

Deterrence

A deterrent is a threat of retaliation in response to a given act, in other words, making the consequences of an act less desirable to the potential perpetrators.

Examples might include economic or political sanctions, legal action, disengagement and consequent exclusion of the perpetrators from various benefits. Deterrence can also include armed response although this is not an option available to most travellers.

A strategy of deterrence has several limitations. The implementers of the strategy must be both able to carry out the threatened response and be perceived to be able to do this by the people it is intended to deter. The perpetrators must understand the deterrent *before* they commit the offence.

Another common problem with deterrence is that innocent victims may be harmed if it is not possible to target the retaliation precisely. For example, an entire community may be affected by sanctions rather than just the individuals who committed an offence.

Retaliation may simply lead to a worsening of a problem with both sides increasingly threatening.

RISK MANAGEMENT

Risk management is the process of assessing how likely it is that you, or those you are responsible for, will be affected by a particular set of dangers and putting measures in place to reduce either the chances of a danger affecting you or reducing its impact if it does happen. Being able to respond to unexpected events may also be considered a part of this process.

The questions to be considered are straightforward. There can, however, be a tendency to make risk management more complicated than it needs to be, this is best avoided.

The stages of risk management:

For a given environment evaluate the following:

- What are the Dangers?
- Who is at risk?
- How can I reduce the level of risk?
- What risks do I still have to live with?
- What can I do if something does go wrong?

Acceptance of risk

Having looked at your options for managing risk, it is important to ask yourself if it is safe enough to travel to your destination. Individuals and organisations will have different views on what is an acceptable level of risk. It is important that these differences are resolved before travelling to a potentially hazardous environment.

DANGERS, HAZARDS & THREATS

Many people misunderstand what is meant by 'risk'. There are many dangers* but we are not all equally exposed to them.

To assess your level of risk, you must:

- Identify potential dangers
- Ask how *likely* it is that this danger will affect you?
- Ask how bad the consequences would be?

Risk is therefore an assessment of the *likelihood & impact* of an incident were it to happen to a particular person or group of people. Danger and risk are not the same thing, for example, a meteorite would be dangerous if it hit you on the head, but the chances of that actually happening are extremely small and so the risk is also low.

To understand a risk factor, you must answer two questions:

- What is the harm?
- Who would be harmed?

Both likelihood and impact can be affected by personal and situational factors.

*Dangers are sometimes referred to as 'hazards' or 'threats'

Factors affecting exposure to risks

Factors affecting likelihood, e.g.

- Gender
- Age
- Training
- Awareness

Factors affecting impact, e.g.

- Training (e.g. first aid skills)
- Safety equipment (e.g. seatbelts in vehicles)
- Resources (e.g. local medical facilities)

Reducing risk

Reducing risk means either reducing the likelihood of an event happening or its impact if it does. In the case of travelling in a vehicle, options might include the following:

Reducing likelihood

- Driver training
- No driving at night time
- Reducing speed
- Travelling only to certain areas

Reducing Impact

- Wearing seatbelts
- Reducing speed
- First aid training for passengers
- Emergency response plan

Risk assessment

Risk Assessment usually refers to a formal process of evaluating the risks you face. It is an important step in risk management.

Risk assessment should not be complicated!

You do not need to include every risk you can imagine, only those that are particularly dangerous and that may require out of the ordinary knowledge or training to avoid (e.g. for adults: getting kidnapped, yes; running with scissors, no).

Preparing a risk assessment for a given group:

1. Clearly identify, define and distinguish the significant dangers (what is the specific harm?)
2. Evaluate the level of exposure (likelihood)
3. Evaluate how bad it would be if the incident happened (impact)
4. Assess the level of risk by looking at both likelihood and impact

Acceptance of risk

Is the level of risk acceptable? If no, introduce risk reduction measures and re-evaluate risk levels, etc.

STANDARD OPERATING PROCEDURES

Standard operating procedures (S.O.P.'s) are specific activities that form part of a normal routine for ensuring safety (e.g. daily radio checks, logging travel plans, etc.)

S.O.P.'s need to be

- Clear and simple to follow
- Designed with and by the people they will affect
- Understood and valued by the people they apply to
- Enable rather than prevent people achieving their objectives
- Reviewed at appropriate intervals to ensure that they are still relevant
- Monitored to ensure that they are being followed correctly

Dogmatic and irrelevant procedures will quickly be subverted or ignored altogether.

If you are managing a team of people, it is important to take the necessary time to explain why the procedures matter and to ensure a clear understanding of them. In particular, It should be clear that the security measures allow people to function safely in a given area whereas without them it may not be possible or acceptable to operate at all.

CONTINGENCY PLANNING

In the event of an incident occurring, how will you or your organisation respond? This question needs to be answered before a problem occurs. Trying to make things up at the time of an incident is a failure to prepare.

Questions to ask...

- Who could the incident affect?
  - directly
  - indirectly (e.g. family, clients, colleagues)
- Who is responsible for taking decisions?
- What are the lines of communication and will they survive the incident?
- Is there a standby incident management team?
- Do you need a crisis team to manage the impact on the organisation?
- What other authorities might be involved and how will this be coordinated?
- What resources will be needed to deal with the incident?

Another benefit of planning for incidents you can foresee is that many of the same procedures will help you if something happens that you did not anticipate.

NOTES

Use these pages to record important information that you might need in an emergency

EMERGENCY CONTACTS

List contact details for anyone you might need to contact in an emergency:

Name	Contact Details

Index

Preface   1

Travel Safety   3

   Preparing to Go.................................4
   A point of contact.............................5
   Packing for Your Trip.........................6
   Clothing..7
   Air Travel......................................8
   Hotel & Hostel Safety.........................9
   Urban Safety..................................10

Other People   11

   Cultural Differences.........................12
   Building Relationships.......................13
   Managing your team..........................14
   Diffusing Anger..............................15

On the Move   17

   Death & Injury on the Road...................18
   Inspecting a Vehicle.........................19
   Vehicle Equipment............................20
   Driver Skills Check-list.....................21
   Taxis...22
   Buses & Coaches..............................23
   Checkpoints..................................24

Driving In Convoy..26

Armoured Vehicles..27

Crime   29

Tips for Avoiding Crime..30

Sexual Aggression..31

Civil-Unrest..35

Active Shooter Incidents..36

Interviews & Meetings..38

Information Security..39

Avoiding Surveillance..41

Car-Jack..42

Gifts, Bribes & Extortion..44

Abduction & Kidnap..45

Hostile Environments & Weapons of War   49

Surviving Hostile Environments..50

Small Arms Fire..51

Ambush & Crossfire..52

Roadside Bombs..53

Bomb Blasts..54

Grenade Attack..55

Improvised Explosive Devices..56

Explosive Remnants of War..57

Landmines..59

Cluster Bombs..62

Field First Aid 63

Incident Management...64
First Aid Essentials...65
Casualty Report - A.T.M.I.S.T..68
Altitude Sickness...69
Diarrhoea...70
Stress...71
Tear Gas/Water Cannon...73
Malaria...74
Cross Contamination...75

Surviving Natural Disasters 77

Natural Disasters...78
Emergency Evacuation...80
Emergency Shelter...81
Missing Person Card...83
Missing Person...84

Communications 85

Communication Hardware...86
Radio Procedure...88
Common Radio Terms...89
Phonetic Alphabet...90
Incident Reporting...91
Global Positioning Systems (GPS)...92

Appendix 93

Awareness...94

Security Factors...95

Information & Security...96

Understanding The Security Environment...................97

Situational Awareness...98

Actor Mapping...99

Time Lines...100

Putting it all Together..101

Approaches to Security..102

Risk Management..105

Dangers, Hazards & Threats.....................................106

Standard Operating Procedures...............................109

Contingency Planning..110

Notes 111

Emergency Contacts 117

Printed in the United Kingdom

safety@fieldcraft.co.uk

or visit

www.fieldcraft.co.uk